TABLE OF CONTENTS

TABLE OF CONTENTS 1

INTRODUCTION 2

1. SPRING 6

2. SUMMER 23

3. AUTUMN 44

4. WINTER 62

6. WILD ANIMALS 79

SOLUTION – SPRING 96

SOLUTION – SUMMER 98

SOLUTION – AUTUMN 100

SOLUTION – WINTER 102

SOLUTION – WILD ANIMALS 105

INTRODUCTION

Welcome to the Stress Reduction Memory Activity Book for Seniors! This captivating and enjoyable book is crafted to assist seniors in enhancing their memory, stimulating cognitive functions, and achieving relaxation through a range of fun and challenging activities. Inside, you'll discover an exciting array of nature-themed memory games and puzzles, organized around five related themes: Spring, Summer, Autumn, Winter, and Wild Animals.

Each theme presents a variety of engaging games, spanning easy, medium, and difficult levels, thoughtfully designed to cater to diverse interests and keep your mind sharp. Let's delve into some of the thrilling activities awaiting you:

- **Silly Sentences:** In this game, you'll enjoy rearranging scrambled words to form complete and amusing sentences. Showcase your linguistic skills as you decipher and reconstruct these jumbled phrases.
- **Find:** Engage in a scavenger hunt by finding and circling items from a checklist.
- **Find Shadow:** Challenge your visual perception by identifying the correct shadows that match the given images. A sharp eye is essential for success in this delightful task.

- **Going Backward:** Exercise your cognitive flexibility by reading sentences and rewriting them backward on the next page. This playful twist on language keeps your brain agile and adaptable.
- **Memory Challenge:** Put your memory retention to the test with a quick glimpse of words. On the following page, write down as many words as you can remember.
- **What is the End of the Road:** Navigate through paths to determine the correct item name for each end. This activity will challenge your spatial and deductive abilities.
- **Particular Pictures:** Enhance your visual memory by memorizing specific words. Turn the page and identify the items you recall from memory.
- **Charades:** Unleash your creativity with this classic game. Use the given suggestions to come up with answers and enjoy hours of laughter with friends and family.
- **Find the Difference:** Sharpen your observation skills by examining and comparing a series of images. Spot the differences between the pictures.

- **Starts with "...":** Dive into words related to the section's theme, all beginning with the letter "..." This puzzle reinforces memory recall and associations.

Classic Puzzle Games & Brain Games: We've also included a variety of classic puzzles and brain games in this book, such as:

- **Word Search**
- **Crossword**
- **Sudoku**
- **Coloring**

This Stress Relief Memory Activity Book for Seniors is not just a source of entertainment but also a valuable tool to maintain and enhance mental sharpness. Whether you're playing solo or with loved ones, these activities promise joy, relaxation, and a stronger memory.

So, let's embark on this memory-boosting journey together and enjoy the benefits of playful learning! Happy memory exercising!

PUZZLES

01
SPRING

SILLY SENTENCES

Rearrange the scrambled words to make completed sentences.

1. In / song/ of/ the / we / hear / the / of / birdsong / spring / call / arriving

....

....

2. Like / flowers / blooming / hearts / spring / is / a / to / for / expand / people / time / their / and / hopes

....

....

3. Spring / is / a / when / nature / both / moment / and / immerse / themselves / in / humans / rebirth

....

....

4. With / step / under / every / the / life / taken / spring / we / feel / the / awakening / of / sunshine / everywhere

....

....

FIND THE DIFFERES

Circle the 5 differences between the two pictures

GOING BACKWARD

Read this sentence and rewrite it backward on the next page.

> Untie the rope, anchor away from the safe harbor, and let the sails catch the wind. Discover. Dreamy. Detect

MEMORY CHALLENGE

Take one quick look at these words and write as many as you can remember on the next page.

Cherry blossom	Pansy	Tulip	Daisy
Bluebell	Orchid	Rose	Sunflower
Marigold	Peony	Sweet pea	Jasmine

GOING BACKWARD ANSWERS

....

....

....

....

....

....

....

....

....

....

MEMORY CHALLENGE

WHICH PICTURE IS NEXT?

Enter the number of images below at the end to complete the form

1   2   3   4   5   6

WHAT IS IT?

Read the question about the spring theme and guess what it is

Question 1:

Which animal usually appears first in spring and is considered a symbol of this season?

....

....

Question 2:

How many months are there in spring?

....

....

Question 3:

Among spring flowers, which one is usually yellow and a symbol of happiness?

....

....

Question 4:

Spring is an ideal time to do what in the garden?

....

....

MACH WITH THE CORRECT SHADOW

Match the image with the shadow

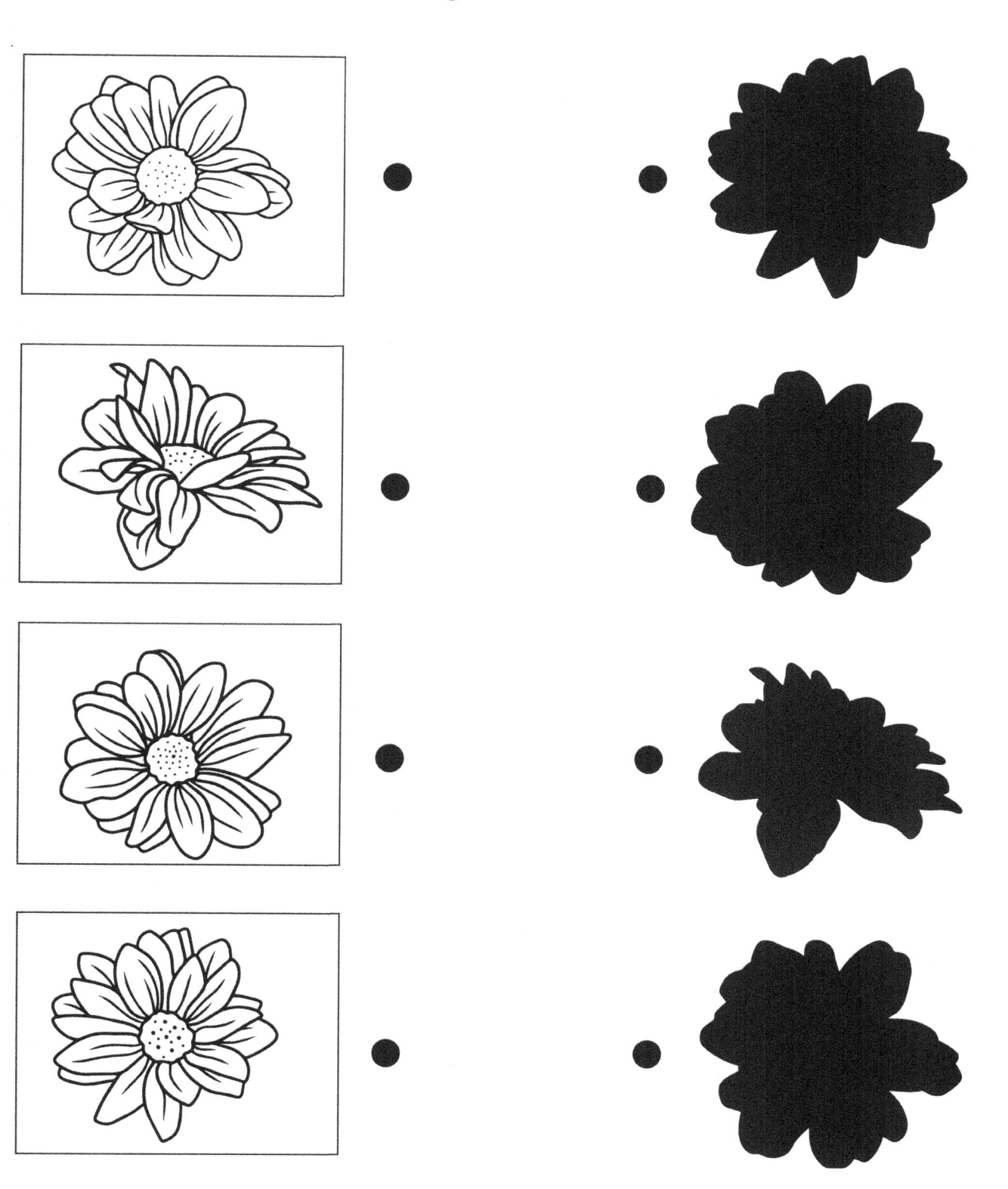

WORD SEARCH

T	M	P	N	T	U	C	N	T	Y	L	I	L	N	S	X	H
C	Q	X	H	R	Y	D	L	R	U	B	Y	S	P	U	U	Y
C	T	W	O	S	P	A	L	V	O	L	L	R	R	Y	B	A
A	C	F	R	Y	P	F	E	V	P	S	I	N	E	G	P	C
R	L	N	U	A	O	F	B	K	C	A	E	P	Q	K	D	I
N	X	J	R	I	P	O	E	W	A	N	N	V	P	P	R	N
A	L	X	E	E	B	D	U	K	M	I	B	S	E	L	X	T
T	T	R	W	X	N	I	L	U	E	F	Y	T	Y	E	S	H
I	P	N	O	A	C	L	B	J	L	A	U	K	M	Q	I	L
O	D	Y	L	I	D	B	M	N	L	N	M	O	A	E	R	O
N	L	N	F	N	D	A	K	J	I	L	R	T	R	C	I	X
K	O	O	N	N	R	U	I	A	A	M	I	E	E	F	P	D
M	G	E	U	I	T	R	J	S	Q	D	T	L	D	X	C	I
V	I	P	S	Z	G	V	H	W	Y	S	K	X	A	D	A	J
H	R	S	L	Q	T	R	W	F	A	N	X	Y	D	C	P	M
B	A	J	Y	C	M	O	R	C	H	I	D	Q	K	B	F	F
E	M	H	A	D	G	V	J	J	Q	L	N	P	C	Q	G	F

ASTER	DAISY	MARIGOLD	POPPY
BLUEBELL	HYACINTH	ORCHID	ROSE
CAMELLIA	IRIS	PANSY	SUNFLOWER
CARNATION	LILAC	PEONY	TULIP
DAFFODIL	LILY	PETUNIA	ZINNIA

CROSSWORD

Across

1. Broccoli ___
5. Curses
10. The "L" of U.N.L.V.
13. Separator of continents
15. Hunter constellation
16. AIDS treatment drug
17. Popular children's book series ... whose protagonist is "hiding" in the circled letters
19. ___ 1 (Me.-to-Fla. highway)
20. Defect
21. Pass without effect, as a storm
23. What corn kernels attach to
25. Beachgoer's shade
27. Where "no one can hear you scream," per "Alien"
28. Now is the winter of ___ discontent ...
29. Alternatively ..., in texts
31. Steve Martin's "King ___"
32. General ___ chicken
34. Westernmost of the Aleutians
36. Immigration or the economy, in a presidential election
40. Tea set?
43. My Name Is ___ Lev
44. Sashimi fish
45. Ye gods!, for one
46. If I Ruled the World rapper

Down

1. Part of an airplane seat assignment
2. Cry in Cologne
3. *Base of many gravies
4. Rank below a marquis
5. ___ Jones Industrials
6. The "A" in U.A.E.
7. Prefix with liter
8. Stop, I beg you!
9. Toddler's winter wear
10. Caterpillar stage, for example
11. Quetzalcoatl worshiper
12. One cubic meter
14. That's swell!
18. Try to hit, as a gnat
22. Decides one will
23. Terra ___ (tile material)
24. Gives the boot to
26. What's ___ like?
30. Start of an encrypted URL address
33. Shorthand takers
35. Salt Lake City native
37. Gathering just for guys
38. Blurt out, perhaps
39. Prefix with -centric
41. Great injustice
42. Organization for Janet Yellen, informally

48. Mets' ballpark until 2008
50. ___-X
51. Recesses
55. Gridiron grp.
56. ___ or con
57. Settles the score
59. Isle of exile
61. Farm-related: Abbr.
62. Title characters in Disney's first full-length feature
66. ___ Death (2000s Fox sitcom)
67. Oak and teak
68. Really bother
69. Yadda, yadda, yadda: Abbr.
70. Busybody
71. ___ Swann, Super Bowl X M.V.P.

47. Extreme
49. For ___ know ...
51. Playing marble
52. For real, in slang
53. PC shortcut for "copy"
54. Complement of Disney dwarfs
58. Onetime competitor of Nair
60. Biblical false god
63. Org. protecting U.S. secrets
64. Enthusiast
65. RR stop

SUDOKU

1	8	2	4	9			3	
6	9			7			2	1
5	3	7	1	8	2	9	4	6
8		3			4	1	5	
	6	1	3	5				
	4				7			
		6	2	3	1		9	8
7		9			5	3	6	2
3					9	4	1	5

COUNTING NUMBERS

Circle the numbers from smallest to largest, starting from 1 to 60

1	49	28	12	20	34	31	5	25	37	8	29
56	10	44	22	60	47	53	41	18	39	14	46
4	40	15	36	2	58	27	55	7	35	42	21
59	54	24	51	30	38	16	48	23	11	32	57
17	45	33	13	6	26	50	43	9	19	52	3

FIND THE NUMBER

Look for the number

1	23	15	17	11		20	10	14	9	4
43	7	6	4	36		15	19	48	41	33
22	5	27	10	24		47	36	12	6	16
9	14	2	29	19		18	11	32	5	3

—— **FIND** ——

11	27	7	19	6

—— **FIND** ——

4	20	14	15	3

FIND THIS OBJECT!

Find and circle FOUR objects in this picture

WRITING ACTIVITES

"Write a short paragraph about your feelings and experiences with spring. Describe how spring brings freshness and hope, and how changes in nature affect your mood and thoughts. Connect your personal experiences with renewal, rejuvenation, or growth in your personal life."

FIND PICTURE

Tick the items used for the SPRING

COLORING

02
SUMMER

SILLY SENTENCES

Rearrange the shuffled words to make a complete sentence and answer it

1. The / outdoor /and / enjoy / night / under / concerts / barbecues / summer / sky

....

....

2. Let / the / space / flowers / up / summer / your / brighten / living

....

....

3. Wake / in / up / morning / day / with / bright / every / faith / a / fresh / day / the / like / summer / sun

....

....

4. Every/ natural/ life/ summer/ scene/ is/ a/ masterpiece/ full/ of/ color/ and / , /

....

....

UNCRAMBLE WORDS

Rearrange the letters and write complete sentences

IMINGMSW TOLFA

___ ___ ___ ___

BLLA

___ ___ ___ ___

NGESSLSSUA

___ ___ ___ ___

CRUNSSNEE

___ ___ ___ ___

GOING BACKWARD

Read this sentence and rewrite it backward on the next page.

In the summer sunshine, life is like a painting, shimmering with golden hues, gentle fragrances, and moments filled with happiness.

MEMORY CHALLENGE

Take one quick look at these words and write as many as you can remember on the next page.

Sun	Ocean	Sandy beach
Sand	Waves	Sunshine
Grassland	Ice cream	Swimming

GOING BACKWARD ANSWERS

MEMORY CHALLENGE

FIND THIS OBJECT!

Find and circle five objects in this picture

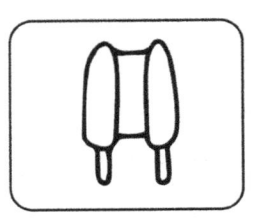   

CHARADES

Use the suggestions below to come up with an answer

- A typical flower of summer with brilliant and bright beauty

- The flowers are large, up to several tens of centimeters in diameter.

- The color of the flower is shiny yellow. When blooming, the flower always faces the rising sun, sometimes people also call it a sun flower.

....

....

- This is an animal that often appears in the summer

- Are considered a symbol of return and hope, as they often return to their breeding grounds each year. Their return is also often seen as a sign of the coming summer, when nature begins to fill with new life after the cold winter.

....

....

PARTICULAR PICTURES

Memorize the image and tick the image to appear on the next page

PARTICULAR PICTURES

Tick on the image that appeared on the previous page

WORD SEARCH

```
T C M B D C Q S D N E K E E W V G
N H H U G F R S Q A S T R O S E R
S U S U R F O U C H E N S E O B D
W C I Q X I C B I O A X M N K U I
X C W S X X W A O S L V Y O U U V
N O O M Y E N O H A E J L M I U E
C E G A Y O V Y X O T P A O X E D
T B R U U I M D N E P S S H Q N D
Y I E U I N R B S E V B T L J O N
X F I I Q U H E S T Q T O E I D A
Y W T G E T A W A Y S W O S W N L
Y X A P C R E G N U O L F E F A S
N I O H O P K L H B P F E V E E I
U P L G C O W E J H H B R A B C O
A G F T E T L F O B V T A W Q O A
F Q J S A N D O R P C K B L D D I
S W I M T K G N S A N D Y E H Q U
```

BAREFOOT   GETAWAYS   POOL   SURF

BOAT   HONEYMOON   RESORTS SWIM

CRUISE   ISLAND   SAND   VOYAGE

DIVE   LOUNGER   SANDY   WAVES

FLOATIER   OCEAN   SPEND   WEEKENDS

SUDOKU

8				9		1	4	
	4	9	2	6				8
		2		5	4	6		9
7		4			6	2		3
2		8		4	7		6	5
	5			1	2		8	7
5	3		4		8		9	6
9		6		7			2	4
4		7	6	3	9		5	1

CROSSWORD

Across

1. Rush!, on an order
5. Bird important in Mayan symbology
10. Effect of the moon's gravity
14. That's ___ ask
15. Heart parts
16. Cousins of ostriches
17. Show some mercy!
19. At the drop of ___ (instantly)
20. Group of gnats
21. Particle with no electric charge
23. What buffalo do in "Home on the Range"
26. Motions left or right on Tinder
27. Secret military operation
32. Heavyweight champ after Liston
33. Peace begins with a ___: Mother Teresa
34. Secret supply
38. Wanton look
40. Precipitous
42. Creme-filled cookie
43. Theme
45. The game is ___: Sherlock Holmes
47. Suffix with different or confident

Down

1. Sounds of satisfaction
2. Cole ___ (side dish)
3. The "A" in Thomas A. Edison
4. Marie Curie's research partner and husband
5. ___-jongg
6. Had something
7. Commercial lead-in to Apple
8. Suffix with zillion
9. 1960s dance craze
10. Rip open
11. Beatnik's "Gotcha"
12. One of the Allman Brothers
13. These: Sp.
18. Winged cupids in art
22. Duos
24. Devices you can bank on, briefly
25. Tiki bar order
27. Smooth, as seas
28. Butterlike spread
29. ___ Cong
30. Like Superman's chin, famously
31. Start 18 holes
35. Puccini's "Nessun dorma," for one
36. Blacken, as a steak
37. Please ___ (operator's request)

48. Perform an act of kindness, in a way
51. Self-conscious question
54. Floating arctic mass
55. Coastal resort areas
58. Longtime name on "Wheel of Fortune"
62. Military sch.
63. *Garnish for a cocktail
66. Hawaii's state bird
67. Wrist/elbow connectors
68. Cincinnati's place
69. ___ shocked as you are
70. Arcade coin
71. River near the Great Pyramids

39. Hazards for offshore swimmers
41. Place to swim
44. Renown
46. Treasure chest
49. Umpire's yell
50. One-third of a Clue accusation
51. Resident of Tehran
52. Words to an attack dog
53. Former Mrs. Trump
56. Guthrie with a guitar
57. Plummeted
59. M*A*S*H soft drink
60. Armstrong who said "The Eagle has landed"
61. Succulent houseplant
64. Scot's refusal
65. Airer of "Family Feud" reruns

COUNTING NUMBERS

Circle the numbers from smallest to largest, starting from 61 to 120

62 107 70 105 100 117 65 119 87 77 72 92

114 91 95 75 80 112 98 103 68 111 83 120

102 67 73 85 89 61 93 115 108 63 99 118

82 110 78 69 81 109 66 96 90 74 106 116

64 86 97 71 76 101 94 104 79 113 84 88

FIND THE NUMBER

Look for the number

42 48 12 3 20 43 9 35 32 28

25 34 2 26 15 8 37 49 5 6

40 13 46 29 44 45 1 22 11 31

7 38 14 33 4 21 17 16 36 18

19 41 24 10 39 30 47 23 50 27

FIND

2 11 1 34 24 8 23 15 41

FIND SHADOW

Find the exact shadow with the original photo

WHAT IS IT?

Read the questions and guess what natural phenomena they are

Question 1:

The gentle face in the morning,
By noon, fierce and glowing, stern and bold.
Come evening, gentle again it seems,
Nightly, hiding amidst clouds, elusive it dreams.
What is it?

Question 2:

There is no bridge across the river
Don't cross streams but climb clouds
Colors yellow, blue, red, purple, bright pink
Guess which bridge it is?

Question 3:

What season is scorching sun,
The sky dazzlingly bright,
Clouds don't even glance,
We must wear hats.

FIND THE DIFFERES

Circle the 5 differences between the two pictures

WRITING ACTIVITES

Write a short paragraph (around 150-200 words) about a special summer experience you've had. You can choose an event such as a trip, a camping excursion, a day at the beach, or any other experience you'd like to share. Use emotions, sensory details, and descriptions to make your paragraph vivid.

Answer the questions.

1. What summer experience did you choose? Why did you choose it?

----

2. In your summer experience, are there any specific memories you'd like to share further?

----

3. If given the chance, would you want to relive the feeling of that summer? Why?

FIND PICTURE

Tick the items used for the SUMMER

COLORING

03
AUTUMN

SILLY SENTENCES

Rearrange the scrambled words to make completed sentences.

. Autumn / like / a / dewdrop / morning / is / bringing / a / of / sense / and / happiness / peace

....
....
....

Let / be / an / autumn / leaf / in / yourself / enjoying / drifting / ⟨e / space / and / life

....
....
....

. is / a / period / of / renewal / Autumn / where / one / transition ⁄ an / feel / the / of / and / beauty / growth

....
....
....

To / autumn / we / of / embrace / to / to / need / life / learn / ⁱange / as / part / see

....
....
....

DOT TO DOT

Connect the points in order to complete the picture.

GOING BACKWARD

Read this sentence and rewrite it backward on the next page.

> Like autumn, our lives also undergo changes, losses. Yet within the fading, there lies the beauty of maturity and depth. Let your heart expand, recognize, and cherish the true values in each moment of life.

MEMORY CHALLENGE

Take one quick look at these words and write as many as you can remember on the next page.

Yellow leaves	Morning dew	Sunrise
Sunset	Cold breeze	Sunlight
Ripened crops	Dry grass	Birdsong

GOING BACKWARD ANSWERS

MEMORY CHALLENGE

FIND THE DIFFERES

Circle the 5 differences between the two pictures

WORD SEARCH

W	E	J	T	O	L	A	O	W	X	I	R	R	P	Q	G	L
S	R	S	T	M	J	T	O	I	P	O	W	O	F	H	D	P
W	U	A	R	J	K	L	U	A	F	P	R	L	Y	E	T	V
R	C	V	O	C	L	B	C	N	T	O	I	O	Y	H	U	H
J	W	J	P	E	I	O	S	E	C	B	L	C	M	N	N	W
Q	M	K	Y	R	R	Q	L	R	Y	M	X	I	O	R	L	D
O	M	B	C	N	C	P	Y	O	J	L	E	S	A	P	A	K
H	M	H	M	L	A	N	L	M	G	J	A	E	N	G	W	D
H	P	P	X	M	A	L	B	A	W	E	Q	K	R	X	E	T
C	M	K	L	V	A	J	L	C	S	A	A	X	P	T	V	J
N	P	D	D	F	H	N	J	Y	S	O	T	I	U	D	Q	K
U	P	T	E	D	U	G	F	S	K	S	N	L	Q	G	B	N
R	R	S	R	W	P	N	C	D	E	S	D	M	Q	R	L	I
C	G	G	F	I	H	K	O	R	W	Q	Q	Y	O	T	U	X
K	Y	N	M	K	F	P	O	R	M	T	Y	W	W	W	Q	Q
F	A	E	L	E	I	F	V	J	T	J	N	G	O	L	D	C
L	R	L	Q	M	L	E	N	W	V	N	F	L	N	S	Y	H

ACORN	ELM	LEAF	SEASON
BIRCH	FALL	MAPLE	SYCAMORE
BROWN	FOLIAGE	OAK	TREE
COLOR	FOREST	RED	WALNUT
CRUNCH	GOLD	RUST	YELLOW

SUDOKU

2		3			7	6	9	
8		6				1		3
9	7	1		3	6		8	4
5	9			6	8	4	3	
	6	8	4	9			5	
7	3			5		9	6	
6		9	3	1	4	5		
4	2	5	8	7		3	1	
3	1			2				

CROSSWORD

Across

1. Lhasa ___ (dog)
5. Largest pelvic bones
9. Time in Manhattan when it's midnight in Montana
14. As ___ on TV
15. One of nine on a Clue board
16. Way to go
17. Dies ___ (hymn)
18. Hawaiian coffee region
19. Bury
20. 40-hour-a-week work
23. Action before crying "You're it!"
24. Plant bristles
25. What wheels do on an axis
27. Yuletide beverage
30. Round-the-campfire treats
32. Studied carefully, with "over"
33. Subject of this puzzle
36. Lord, is ___? : Matthew 26 : 22
37. Davy Crockett died defending it, with "the"
38. Exasperated cry
39. Takes under advisement
42. Maestro Zubin
44. Leave suddenly
45. Drum with a repetitive name
46. Agreeable suck-ups

Down

1. Yeah, like that'll ever happen
2. Lima's locale
3. Diploma feature
4. Very narrow, as a road
5. Peeving
6. Weavers' devices
7. Actress Skye of "Say Anything ..."
8. Key of Beethoven's Symphony No. 7: Abbr.
9. ___ Bridge (former name of New York's R.F.K. Bridge)
10. Got the gold
11. Awesome!
12. Bothered terribly
13. Two-lanes-into-one highway sign
21. Having length and width only, briefly
22. Maine university town
26. President pro ___
27. Of sweeping proportions
28. Attend
29. Emma, do that sexy dance!
30. Steep embankment
31. Honorees on the second Sunday in May
33. Radon or radium: Abbr.
34. Ancient Rome's ___ the Elder

48. California-based oil giant
49. M.D. who may examine the sinuses
50. Oppressive regime
56. Rice-___
58. Getting ___ years
59. Lab assistant in a horror film
60. Gin's partner
61. English pirate captain
62. State north of Calif.
63. Underhanded sort
64. Teeny, informally
65. Signals silently

35. Hoax
37. Hersey's "A Bell for ___"
40. College term: Abbr.
41. Chipping tool
42. Comfy footwear, for short
43. Love or rage
45. In fashion
46. Literature Nobelist William Butler ___
47. Energy company that filed for bankruptcy in 2001
48. Tums targets
51. Trickster of myth
52. Monogram letter: Abbr.
53. Farming prefix
54. ___ the line (obeyed)
55. Energy output units
57. Actress Long of "Boyz N the Hood"

COUNTING NUMBERS

Circle the numbers from smallest to largest, starting from 121 to 18

122 168 144 154 131 166 151 169 125 138 133 171

174 150 141 134 164 146 176 129 157 142 153 147

127 156 130 143 121 140 149 173 163 123 159 165

137 172 162 136 160 170 132 155 145 135 175 179

180 178 124 167 158 126 152 139 177 128 161 148

FIND THE NUMBER

Look for the number

6	11	2	17	8		2	10	14	9	4
12	7	1	4	16		15	19	3	1	13
13	5	18	10	3		7	17	12	6	16
9	14	15	20	19		18	11	20	5	8

———— **FIND** ————   ———— **FIND** ————

3   5   7   8   16   6   7   13   15   19

COUNTING

Carefully count each type of suitcase and put the total in the space provided.

READ AND ANSWER THE QUESTIONS

Read the short text below and complete the questions.

AUTUMN WEATHER

Autumn arrives, and the scenery becomes more impressive than ever. The golden rays of sunlight stretch across the trees, creating a magical picture of autumn. The leaves turn into vibrant shades of yellow, red, and orange. The sky is clear blue, and the gentle breeze sways the falling leaves, creating the gentle music of autumn. The occasional light rain makes the air more pleasant, cleanses the summer dust, and creates a distinct fragrance of autumn.

Read the text again and answer the questions.

What aspects of autumn scenery are mentioned in the passage?

. Which colors stand out in autumn according to the
assage?

What emotion does the passage describe when
ılking about autumn?

Describe an emotion when one sees the autumn
cenery as in the passage.

WHAT IS THE END OF THE ROAD?

Match two matching images together

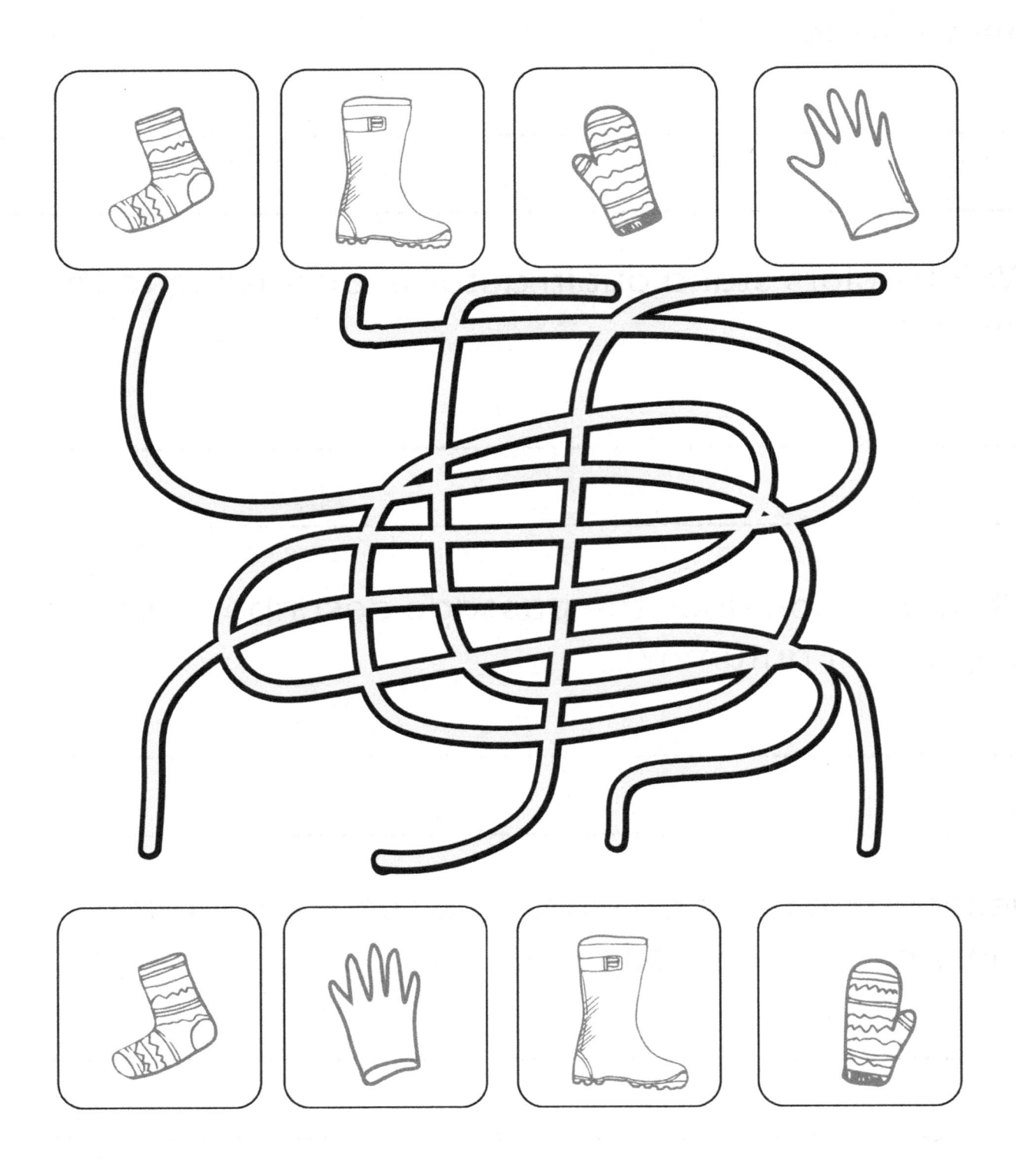

WRITING ACTIVITES

Do you have any special memories during the fall?
Please share about it

....

....

....

....

....

....

....

....

....

....

....

....

....

FIND THIS OBJECT!

Find and circle FOUR objects in this picture

  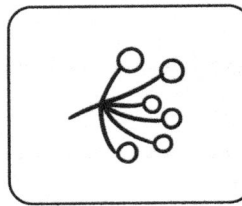 

COLORING

04

WINTER

SILLY SENTENCES

Rearrange the scrambled words to make completed sentences.

1. The / long / of / are / winter / a / wonderful / coffee / nights / time / to / sit / drink / by / the / fire / and/ share / stories / , /

....

....

2. Only / winter / after / can / one / of / experiencing / truly / appreciate / value / the / spring

....

....

3. Every / falling / snowflake / the / is / from / a / sky / promise / freshness / of / discovery / and

....

....

4. No / cold / it / gets / a / matter / how / can / melt / smile / any / heart

....

....

GOING BACKWARD

Read this sentence and rewrite it backward on the next page.

Winter is the time to look back at the past and think about the future, to be grateful for what has passed and hopeful for what is to come.

MEMORY CHALLENGE

Take one quick look at these words and write as many as you can remember on the next page.

Snow	Wind	Fog
Bonfire	Wool	Snowboarding
Warm clothes	Snowfall	Common cold

GOING BACKWARD ANSWERS

MEMORY CHALLENGE

FIND THE SAME PICTURE

Circle the image that resembles the original image

WORD SEARCH

```
L F S N X U L D C N G L U S Y H O
A A F A Q U P K R K D E L S B E U
S Y T G B J M N O O N P P S V E R
T S Y G I G U B S J L F R G D S C
R N S O A N J E S Y U R C H F L F
O O Y B T Y S E I X E B U R I E X
P W K O H S Y A N Y V O F C K D V
S B N T L S D B G I M B H P W D H
I O M F O V S K A O P S P D S I D
N A I X N V D K G C E L E E A N E
T R G G O Q R U I U H E A U R G J
H D C M O J L Q V T P D T N E G B
M S L G W G Y I U S O N R I T B Y
K V U O R P Y E K C O H C C A E L
V E G I N K G O X H X E V P K G R
R Q E T S W O N S P S O V U S K L
N J V K G X V W H D M O L A L S F
```

ALPINE	HOCKEY	SKATE	SNOW
BIATHLON	ICE	SKI	SNOWBOARD
BOBSLED	JUMP	SLALOM	SPEED
CROSSING	LUGE	SLED	SPORTS
CURL	MOGUL	SLEDDING	TOBOGGAN

SUDOKU

6			7		4		9	1
	9	2				8	4	
	1	8	6			7		
2		6		7	5			4
5	7	4		9		3	8	
	8	1	2					7
1		5	9			6	7	8
	2					1	5	9
	6	9	5		7		2	3

CROSSWORD

Across

1. Washboard muscles
4. Yachtsman, e.g.
10. Economist Smith who coined the term "invisible hand"
14. Org. that sticks to its guns?
15. As originally placed
16. Prefix with morphosis
17. Texas, Louisiana, Mississippi, Alabama and Florida
19. M*A*S*H soft drink
20. The Time Machine race
21. ___ Mae (Whoopi's role in "Ghost")
22. Suffix in many English county names
24. Actress Téa of "Fun With Dick and Jane"
26. Venom neutralizer, e.g.
29. ___ Falls, N.Y.
31. Dorm figs.
32. Suffix with expert
33. Venus's sister with a tennis racket
36. Within: Prefix
37. 1992 Tarantino crime thriller
41. Sit for a painting
42. Crankcase reservoir
43. Meas. of a country's economic output

Down

1. Shapes made in the snow
2. Crème ___ (dessert)
3. Swinging-door establishment
4. Ones not entirely gay or straight
5. Hip about
6. Carne ___ (burrito filler)
7. Mythical giant
8. Somme summer
9. Moscow's land
10. Prenatal procedure, informally
11. Road sign that hints at what can be found three times in this puzzle's grid
12. Ones in disbelief?
13. ___ tai (cocktail)
18. Risky bridge play
23. Shaker ___, O.
25. Drink that can cause brain freeze
27. One might be made of bread crumbs
28. Recent: Prefix
30. Flight board abbr.
34. Bring to mind
35. There is ___ in 'team'
36. Wa-a-a-ay in the past

The crossword grid is numbered as follows.

Across/Down clues:

44. Pose a question
46. The deal went through!
50. Junk pile
54. One side of a Faustian bargain
55. Eaglet's nest
56. Dr. ___, Eminem mentor
58. Richard of "Chicago"
59. Rear end, to Brits
60. Futuristic mode of transportation in the "Back to the Future" films
63. Mini-plateau
64. Conundrum
65. Ryan of "When Harry Met Sally ..."
66. Duos
67. Insert a new cartridge
68. Jeanne d'Arc, e.g.: Abbr.

37. Only major-league player to enter the 3,000-hit club in the 1980s
38. Order of coffee in a small cup
39. Engineering sch. in Troy, N.Y.
40. Jamie Foxx's "Yep ___ Me"
41. Printing units: Abbr.
44. Bee: Prefix
45. Common pronoun pairing
47. First-string squads
48. Setting for much of "La Bohème"
49. Feeling anxious
51. Floor measurements
52. Ibuprofen brand
53. Alternative to Ragú
57. Bombeck who wrote "Housework, if you do it right, will kill you"
59. Tsp. or tbsp.
61. Singleton
62. Naughty

FIND THE NUMBER

Find the largest number

170 142 136 155 145 138 125 169 144 171 168 131

174 150 141 134 164 146 176 129 157 151 153 180

127 123 130 143 121 140 149 173 163 156 159 165

137 172 162 166 160 122 132 154 133 135 175 179

147 178 124 167 158 126 152 139 177 128 161 148

COUNTING NUMBERS

Circle the numbers from smallest to largest, starting from 181 to 240

194 218 188 202 233 222 207 192 215 220 196 184

225 182 213 224 199 230 227 186 205 209 190 236

204 191 221 212 216 181 229 195 211 234 200 239

231 185 210 201 235 223 208 232 214 193 217 240

197 228 206 238 189 219 226 183 198 203 187 237

FILL IN THE BLANKS

Fill in the blanks with missing letters

PULLO_ER SO_K HA_ S_ARF _ITTEN

WEATHER MATCHING
Match words suitable to the weather

Stormy

Lightning

Sunny

Foggy

Partly cloudy

Hailing

Blizzard

Sleet

Thunderstorm

Rainbow

Windy

Cloudy

Rainy

Snowy

HOW MANY?

FIND THE CORRECT SHADOW

Let's find the shadow that corresponds to the orginal image

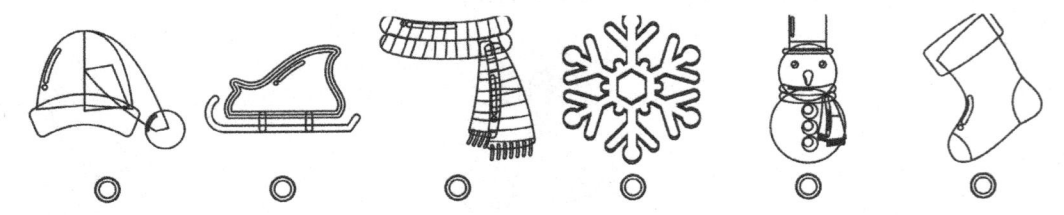

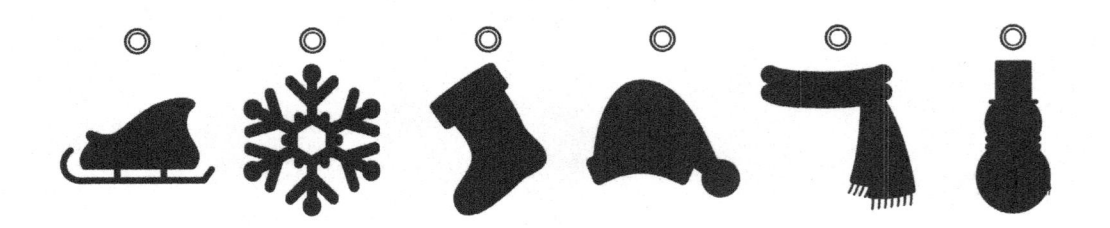

FIND THE CORRECT SHADOW

Let's find the shadow that corresponds to the orginal image

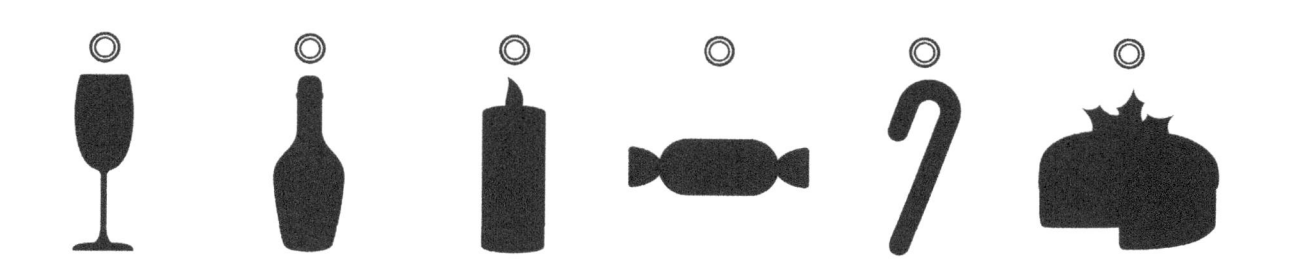

FIND THE CORRECT SHADOW

Let's find the shadow that corresponds to the orginal image

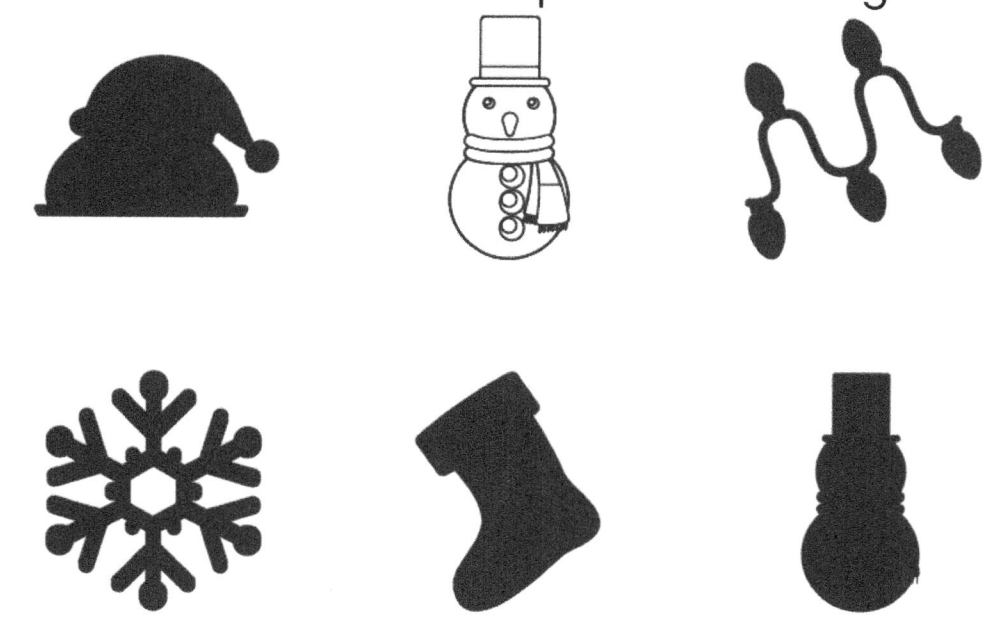

STARTS WITH "C"

In this memory puzzle, the answer to each clue begins with the letter "C" and relates to the "winter" theme of this section

1. festival commemorating the birth of Jesus, held mainly on December 25 every year

....

2. small and crispy cakes, usually made from a mixture of butter, sugar, flour and other ingredients such as vanilla, nuts or chocolate.

....

3 This is the body state when the temperature drops significantly.

....

4. This is an important part of the heating system that, like a duct, carries smoke from the fireplace or fireplace out of the house.

....

HOW MANY ARE THERE?

Look at the picture and count how many pine trees there are

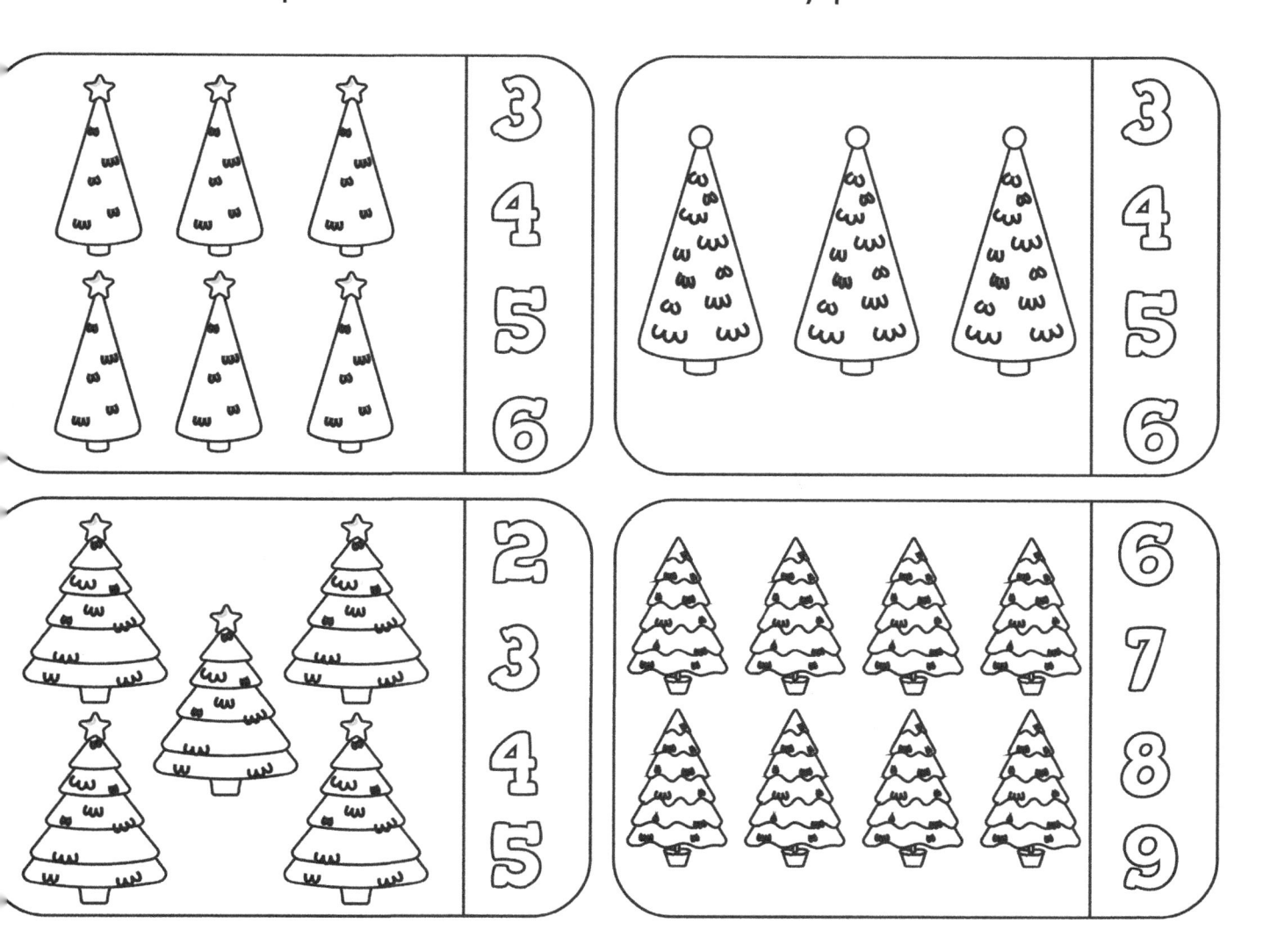

WRITING ACTIVITES

Write about your favorite winter activities, like going skiing
watching the snowfall, or cooking warm meals.

05
WILD ANIMALS

SILLY SENTENCES

Rearrange the scrambled words to make completed sentences.

1. No / to / protect / action / meaningful / wildlife / is / too / small / wildlife/ every / action / is / ,

....

....

2. The / of / Africa / are / survival / savannas / populated / by/ hyenas / lions / and / in / a / cheetahs / perpetual / engaged / struggle / for / ,

....

....

3. Tigers / their / striped / in / known / distinctive / coats / are / among / the / largest / cats / for / the / world

....

....

4. The / forests / the / Northwest / of / are / bald / home / to / grizzly / bears / lush / eagles / Pacific / an/ salmon / and

....

....

GOING BACKWARD

Read this sentence and rewrite it backward on the next page.

> Environmental destruction not only harms wild animals but also threatens the global ecological balance. Conserving wildlife is not only our obligation but also an endeavor to safeguard the precious heritage of the future.

MEMORY CHALLENGE

Take one quick look at these words and write as many as you can remember on the next page.

Wolf	Tigress	Dolphin	Giraffe
Penguin	Rhino	Zebra	Jaguar
Orangutan	Giraffe	Gazelle	Ostrich

GOING BACKWARD ANSWERS

....

....

....

....

....

....

....

....

....

....

MEMORY CHALLENGE

MATCH WORDS WITH CORRECT PICTURE

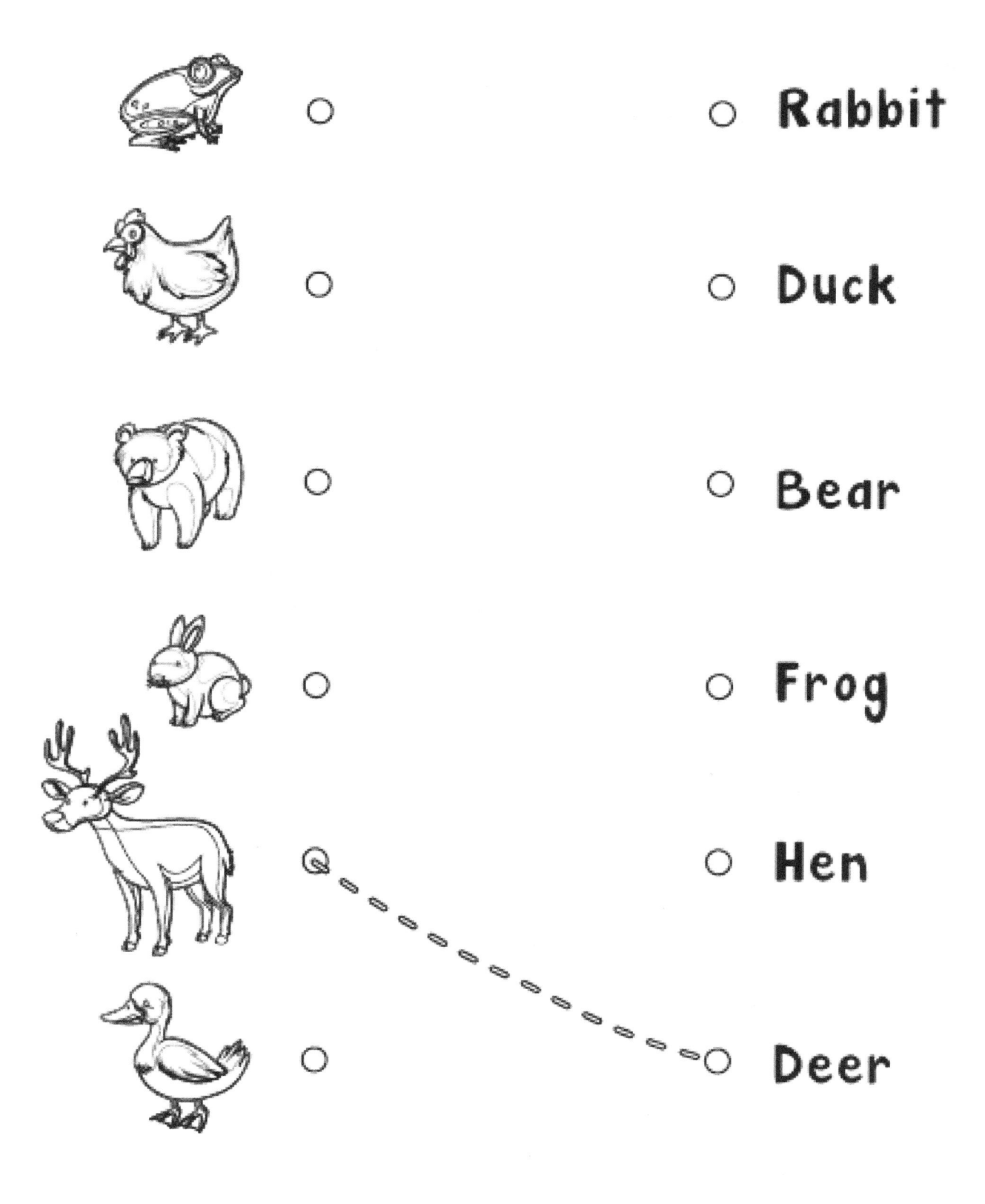

Rabbit

Duck

Bear

Frog

Hen

Deer

WHAT IS IT?

Read the question and guess what animal it is

Question 1:

What animal can jump the farthest in the world?

....

Question 2:

Which animal gives birth without having to carry the pregnancy?

....

Question 3:

What animal can change the color of its body to adapt to its surroundings?

....

Question 4:

What animal can smell from a very far distance?

....

Question 5:

What animal can fly the highest?

....

FILL IN THE BLANKS

Look at the picture and complete the missing words

___ion

___eer

___at

___utterfly

___orilla

___orse

___en

___rab

___at

___urtle

MATCH CORRECT PICTURES

Look at the pictures and connect them together to match
each animal in the picture

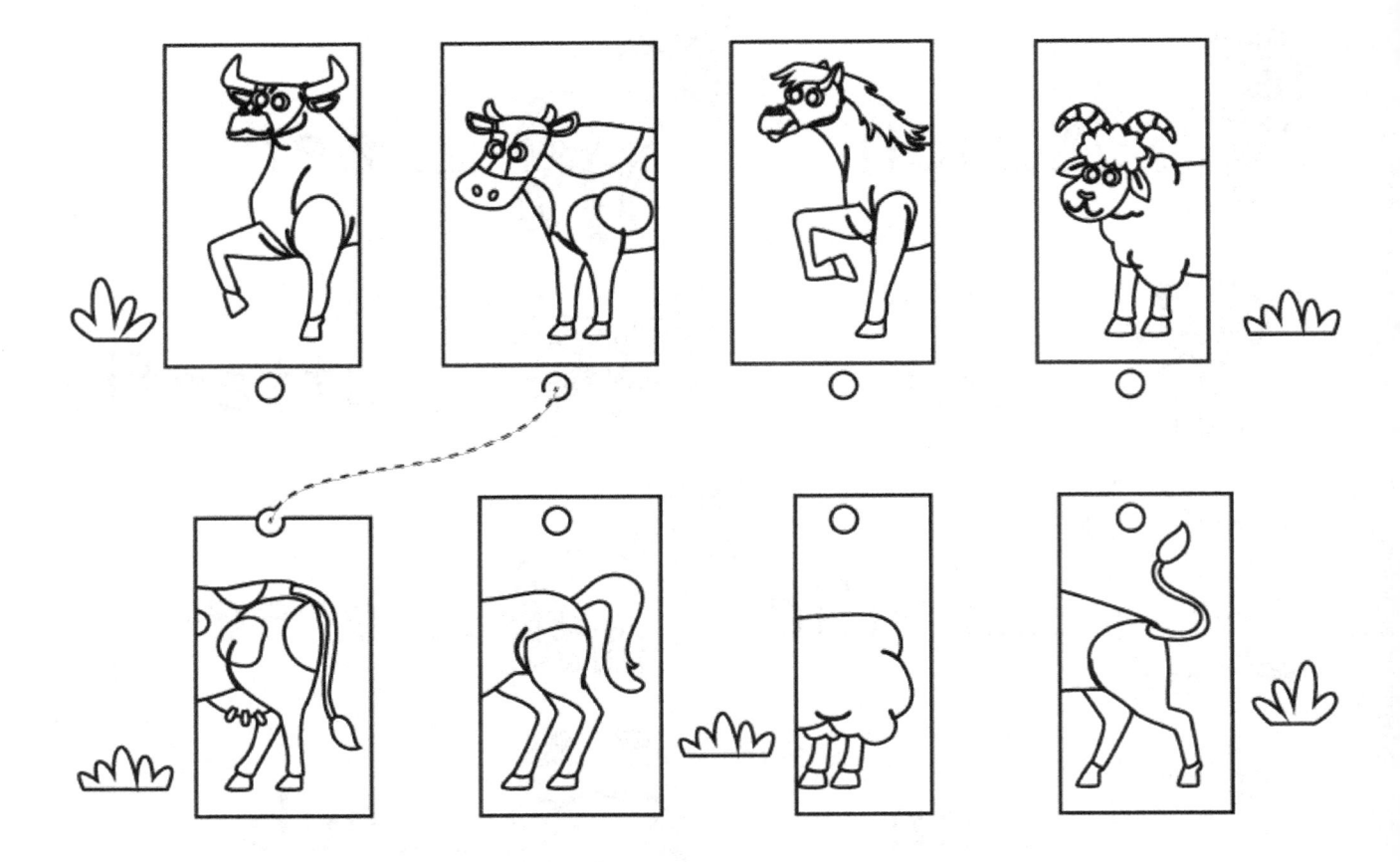

WORD SEARCH

```
G O W X T L A E S B G O K C T U L
A C J O Y G G Y E S L S G R X L C
L E G S G I L A I Y E U W I S T G
C A M U B D R N B E O M H M N X U
K R I B W R U A Y L P A L T A J N
O N O O W I D L P E A T E E K L K
S N L U D G Y L R P R O O S E S M
O F H X E G Q F E H D P P H N Q O
M D K R W W P E G A R O A V C U N
Q A P C K E E E I N E P R R W I K
T D U G X P N T T T K P D N D R E
L N R A H O G A R S X I J E G R Y
V O V T W L U N G K F H E U Y E A
Y I B T W E I A B J D R D L G L H
D L X P L T N M B A Q K U Q S Y E
V V P O P N D O U I S I T D J D I
F O N Y F A Q V P A N D A G E J S
```

ANTELOPE	FOX	LION	SEAL
BADGER	GIBBON	MANATEE	SNAKE
BEAR	HIPPOPOTAMUS	MONKEY	SQUIRREL
DEER	LEOPARD	PANDA	TIGER
ELEPHANT	LEOPARD	PENGUIN	WOLF

SUDOKU

	9			8	5	6	7	
		6			3	1	8	5
8	3	5		6	1		9	
2	4			7		5	1	6
7	5		2	4		9	3	8
6			5		9	7		2
3		7		9		8		
			8	5	2			
		8	1			4	2	

CROSSWORD

Across

1. Enjoy immensely
6. Seethe
10. Part of P.O. or P.S.
14. Kitchen magnet?
15. Parks who received the Presidential Medal of Freedom
16. Persian Gulf leader
17. Green energy source that might go on top of a house
19. First word in many a fairy tale
20. Reverse of WSW
21. Winter Autobahn hazard
22. Eagles' nests
24. Tennis great with a sister who's also a tennis great
28. Thou ___ not ...
30. Kawasaki competitor
31. Claws savagely
32. Hindu queen
33. Ending with Wolf, Bat or Super
36. Paris suburb
37. Bygone music collection from Nas or Lil' Kim
39. One who delights in starting fires, informally
40. Gun, in old mob slang
41. ___ Millions (multistate lottery)

Down

1. Zap with a light beam
2. Elvis's middle name
3. Olympic event for which the world record stands at a little over 20 feet
4. Thurman of Hollywood
5. Mom and dad
6. Shrill and blaring, as a trumpet
7. Suffix with ball
8. Suffix with expert
9. Dreamy state
10. Will it play in ___?
11. ___ vincit amor
12. Words to an attack dog
13. Lock of hair
18. More, to a musician
23. For grades 1-12
25. For Better or for Worse mom
26. On the ___ (incensed)
27. Computer that runs OS X
28. Pollution that may sting the eyes
29. ___-kiri
33. Comment made when itching to leave a dull party
34. Suffix with buck
35. What "n." means in a dictionary

42. Vowel run
43. Former New York senator Alfonse
45. Betray, as a naughty sibling
46. Not-so-fancy places to stay
50. Old Turkish pooh-bahs
51. A.L. West team, on scoreboards
52. Annoying feature of an online stream
55. Hayworth of "Cover Girl"
56. Going in side-by-side pairs
60. State forcefully
61. Rank below a marquis
62. We agree
63. Dickens's Uriah ___
64. Flightless bird of South America
65. Small, secluded valleys

37. Do a new production of, as a recording
38. Actor John of "Sands of Iwo Jima"
39. Ring, as bells
41. Spydom's ___ Hari
42. Floor cover that doesn't reach the walls
43. E flat equivalent on a piano
44. So fancy!
46. The "O" of O magazine
47. Artless
48. ___ Lauder cosmetics
49. Indent key
53. Unto us ___ is given: Isaiah
54. Old Pontiac muscle cars
57. Cartoonish baby cry
58. Metal in a mountain
59. Course for some immigrants: Abbr.

JOIN THE WORDS

Based on the picture and suggested letters, combine them into complete words

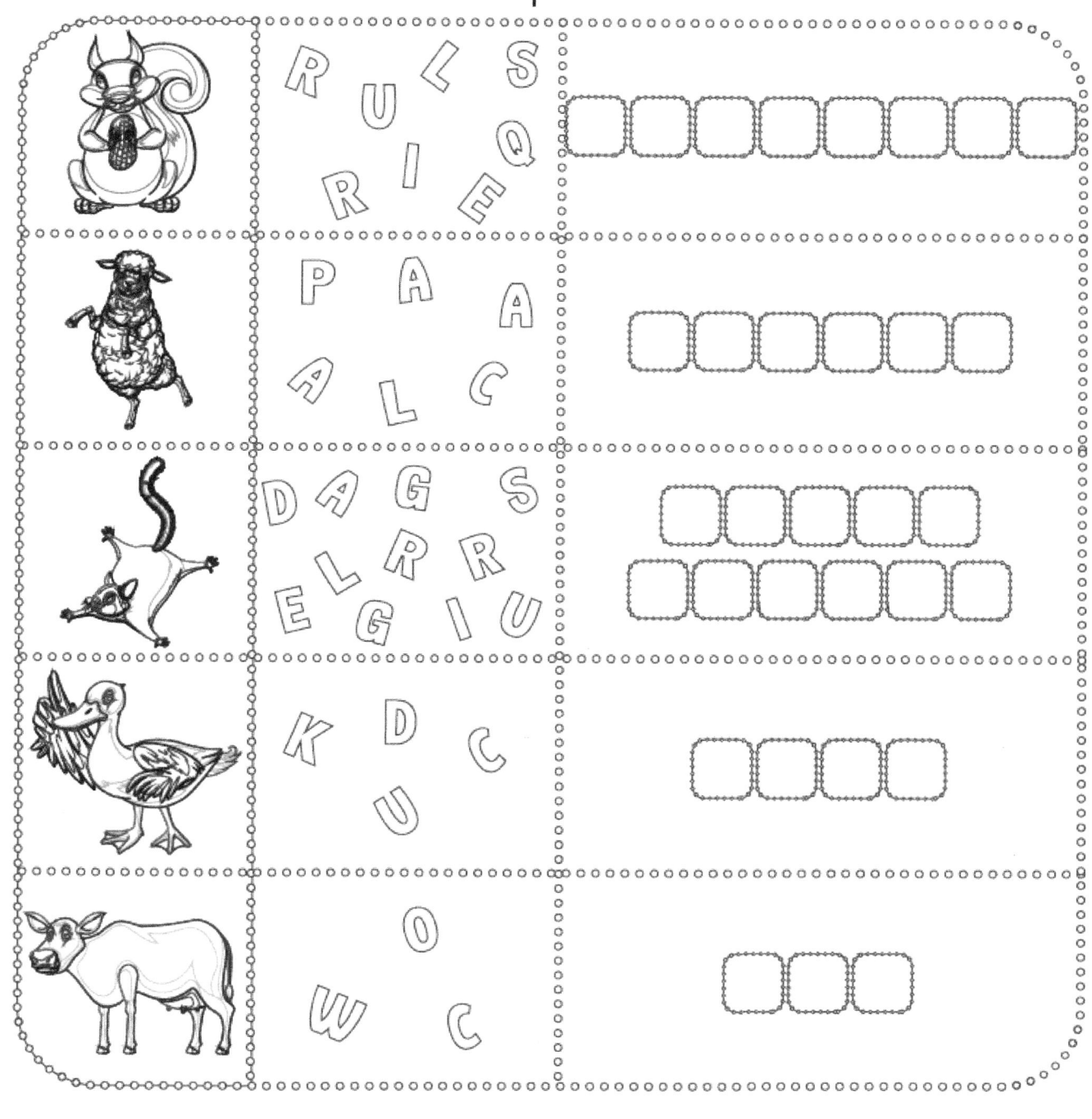

91

FIND THE NUMBER

Find the largest number

15	79	54	27	83	74	92	97	29	17
73	45	19	85	23	82	32	52	68	86
91	22	31	67	14	87	21	80	25	94
24	50	44	28	64	53	46	18	84	60
95	16	81	20	98	30	77	90	96	26

COUNTING NUMBERS

Circle the numbers from smallest to largest, starting from 241 to 300

277	265	270	262	285	297	247	294	282	274	259	245
293	244	249	280	267	272	290	257	242	296	268	288
255	275	260	287	241	279	276	252	292	254	284	278
299	251	289	253	298	264	256	300	263	250	266	271
283	246	273	258	269	291	248	281	261	286	243	295

MATCHING GAME

Look to see which animal these tails belong to and connect them accordingly

FIND THE CORRECT SHADOW

HOW MANY

Count the number of animals in the picture and fill in the number in the blank box

WRITING ACTIVITES

Discuss the meaning and role of each individual in wildlife conservation. Please share your thoughts and action plans to contribute to this conservation effort from a personal perspective.

SOLUTION - SPRING

Silly Sentences

1. In the song of birdsong, we hear the call of spring arriving
2. Like blooming flowers, spring is a time for people to expand their hearts and hopes.
3. Spring is a moment when both nature and humans immerse themselves in rebirth.
4. With every step taken under the spring sunshine, we feel the awakening of life everywhere.

FIND THE DIFFERES

Circle the 5 differences between the two pictures

What is this

1. Bird
2. Three months
3. Daisy
4. Planting flowers

Word Search

T	M	P	N	T	U	C	N	T	Y	L	I	L	N	S	X	H
C	Q	X	H	R	Y	D	L	R	U	B	Y	S	P	U	U	Y
C	T	W	O	S	P	A	L	V	O	L	L	R	R	Y	B	A
A	C	F	R	Y	P	F	E	P	S	I	N	E	G	P	A	C
R	L	N	U	A	O	F	B	K	C	A	E	P	Q	K	D	I
N	X	J	R	I	P	O	E	W	A	N	N	V	P	P	R	N
A	L	X	E	E	B	D	U	K	M	I	B	S	E	L	X	T
T	T	R	W	X	N	I	L	U	E	F	Y	T	Y	E	S	H
I	P	N	O	A	C	L	B	J	L	A	U	K	M	Q	I	L
O	D	Y	L	I	D	B	M	N	L	N	M	O	A	E	R	O
N	L	N	F	N	D	A	K	J	I	L	R	T	R	C	I	X
K	O	O	N	N	R	U	I	A	A	M	I	E	F	P	D	
M	G	E	U	I	T	R	J	S	Q	D	T	L	D	X	C	I
V	I	P	S	Z	G	V	H	W	Y	S	K	X	A	D	A	J
H	R	S	L	Q	T	R	W	F	A	N	X	Y	D	C	P	M
B	A	J	Y	C	M	O	R	C	H	I	D	Q	K	B	F	F
E	M	H	A	D	G	V	J	J	Q	L	N	P	C	Q	G	F

SUDOKU

1	8	2	4	9	6	5	3	7
6	9	4	5	7	3	8	2	1
5	3	7	1	8	2	9	4	6
8	7	3	6	2	4	1	5	9
9	6	1	3	5	8	2	7	4
2	4	5	9	1	7	6	8	3
4	5	6	2	3	1	7	9	8
7	1	9	8	4	5	3	6	2
3	2	8	7	6	9	4	1	5

SOLUTION - SPRING

WHICH PICTURE IS NEXT?

Please enter the number of the images below in the outermost box to complete the pattern

	1
	2
	4
	5
	6

1 2 3 4 5 6

FIND THIS OBJECT!

Find and circle FOUR objects in this picture

MACH WITH THE CORRECT SHADOW

Match the figure with its exact shadow

FIND PICTURE

Tick the items used for the SPRING

Crossword

1 R	2 A	3 B	4 E			5 D	6 A	M	8 N	9 S		10 L	11 A	12 S
13 O	C	E	A	14 N		15 O	R	I	O	N		16 A	Z	T
17 W	H	E	R	E	18 S	W	A	L	D	O		19 R	T	E
			20 F	L	A	W		21 B	L	O	W	22 O	V	E	R
23 C	24 O	B		25 T	A	26 N		27 I	N	S	P	A	C	E
28 O	U	R		29 O	T	O	30 H		31 T	U	T			
32 T	S	O	33 S		34 A	T	T	35 U		36 I	S	37 S	38 U	39 E
40 T	T	T	T	41 T	T	T	T	T	T	42 T	T	T	T	T
43 A	S	H	E	R		44 O	P	A	H		45 O	A	T	H
			46 N	A	47 S		48 S	H	E	49 A		50 G	E	N
51 A	52 L	53 C	O	V	E	54 S		55 N	F	L		56 P	R	O
57 G	E	T	S	E	V	E	58 N		59 E	L	60 B	A		
61 A	G	R		62 S	E	V	E	63 N	D	W	A	R	64 F	65 S
66 T	I	L		67 T	R	E	E	S		68 E	A	T	A	T
69 E	T	C		70 Y	E	N	T	A		71 L	Y	N	N

SOLUTION - SUMMER

Silly Sentences

1. Enjoy outdoor barbecues and concerts under the summer night sky.
2. Let the summer flowers brighten up your living space.
3. Wake up each day with faith in a fresh, bright day, like the summer morning sun.
4. Every summer scene is a natural masterpiece, full of color and life.

UNCRAMBLE WORDS

Rearrange the letters to make a completsenten

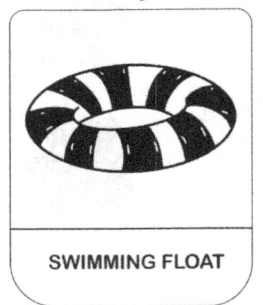

SWIMMING FLOAT

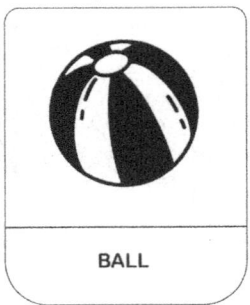

BALL

SUNGLASSES

SUNSCREEN

FIND THIS OBJECT!

Find and circle five objects in this picture

What is this

1. Sun
2. Rainbow
3. Summer

Charades

1. Sunflower,
2. Swallow

Word Search

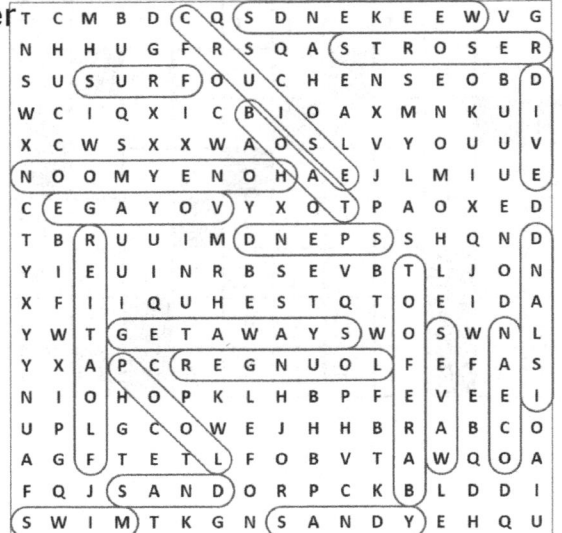

SUDOKU

8	6	5	7	9	3	1	4	2
3	4	9	2	6	1	5	7	8
1	7	2	8	5	4	6	3	9
7	9	4	5	8	6	2	1	3
2	1	8	3	4	7	9	6	5
6	5	3	9	1	2	4	8	7
5	3	1	4	2	8	7	9	6
9	8	6	1	7	5	3	2	4
4	2	7	6	3	9	8	5	1

SOLUTION - SUMMER

PARTICULAR PICTURES
"Fill in the correct sequence numbers for the corresponding mnemonic images from the previous page in the boxes"

FIND SHADOW
Let's find the shadow that corresponds to the original image.

FIND PICTURE
Tick the items used for the SUMMER

FIND THE DIFFERES
Circle the 5 differences between the two pictures

Crossword

1 A	2 S	3 A	4 P		5 M	6 A	7 C	8 A	9 W		10 T	11 I	12 D	13 E
14 A	L	L	I		15 A	T	R	I	A		16 E	M	U	S
17 H	A	V	E	18 A	H	E	A	R	T		19 A	H	A	T
20 S	W	A	R	M		21 N	E	U	22 T	R	I	N	O
			23 R	O	24 A	25 M		26 S	W	I	P	E	S
27 C	28 O	29 V	E	R	T	A	30 C	31 T	I	O	N		
32 A	L	I		33 S	M	I	L	E		34 S	T	35 A	36 S	37 H
38 L	E	E	39 R		40 S	T	E	E	41 P		42 O	R	E	O
43 M	O	T	I	44 F		45 A	F	O	O	46 T		47 I	A	L
			48 P	A	49 Y	I	T	F	O	R	50 W	A	R	D
51 I	52 S	53 I	T	M	E			54 F	L	O	E		
55 R	I	V	I	E	R	56 A	57 S			58 V	A	59 N	60 N	61 A
62 A	C	A	D		63 O	R	A	64 N	65 G	E	P	E	E	L
66 N	E	N	E		67 U	L	N	A	S		68 O	H	I	O
69 I	M	A	S		70 T	O	K	E	N		71 N	I	L	E

99

SOLUTION - AUTUMN

Silly Sentences

1. Autumn is like a morning dewdrop, bringing a sense of peace and happiness.
2. Let yourself be like an autumn leaf, drifting in space and enjoying life.
3. Autumn is a period of transition, where one can sense the beauty of renewal and growth.
4. To embrace autumn, we need to learn to see change as part of life.

FIND THE DIFFERES

Circle the 5 differences between the two pictures

Word Search

W	E	J	T	O	L	A	O	W	X	I	R	R	P	Q	G	L

SUDOKU

2	4	3	1	8	7	6	9	5
8	5	6	9	4	2	1	7	3
9	7	1	5	3	6	2	8	4
5	9	2	7	6	8	4	3	1
1	6	8	4	9	3	7	5	2
7	3	4	2	5	1	9	6	8
6	8	9	3	1	4	5	2	7
4	2	5	8	7	9	3	1	6
3	1	7	6	2	5	8	4	9

SOLUTION - AUTUMN

Read and answer the questions

1. Autumn scenery includes golden sunlight, leaves turning yellow, red, and orange, clear blue sky, and occasional light rain.
2. Yellow, red, and orange colors stand out in autumn.
3. The passage describes a sense of wonder and appreciation for the beauty and tranquility of autumn.
4. An emotion when one sees the autumn scenery could be delight, peace, or excitement with the beauty of nature.

FIND THIS OBJECT!

Find and circle FOUR objects in this picture

Crossword

¹A	²P	³S	⁴O		⁵I	⁶L	⁷I	⁸A		⁹T	¹⁰W	¹¹O	¹²A ¹³M

(crossword grid with filled answers: APSO, ILIA, TWOAM; SEEN, ROOM, ROUTE; IRAE, KONA, INTER; FULLTIMEJOB, TAG; AWNS, ROTATE; EGGNOG, SMORES; PORED, ECONOMICS; ITI, ALAMO, GAH; CONSIDERS, MEHTA; DECAMP, TOMTOM; YESMEN, ARCO; ENT, POLICESTATE; ARONI, ONIN, IGOR; TONIC, KIDD, OREG; SNEAK, ITSY, NODS)

COUNTING

Carefully count each type of suitcase and put the total in the space provided.

 **6**    **8**    **4**    **6**

SOLUTION - WINTER

Silly Sentences

1. The long nights of winter are a wonderful time to sit by the fire, drink coffee, and share stories.
2. Only after experiencing winter can one truly appreciate the value of spring.
3. Every snowflake falling from the sky is a promise of freshness and discovery.
4. No matter how cold it gets, a smile can melt any heart.

Find the largest number

170	142	136	155	145	138	125	169	144	171	168	131
174	150	141	134	164	146	176	129	157	151	153	**180**
127	123	130	143	121	140	149	173	163	156	159	165
137	172	162	166	160	122	132	154	133	135	175	179
147	178	124	167	158	126	152	139	177	128	161	148

Word Search

Sudoku

6	5	3	7	8	4	2	9	1
7	9	2	3	5	1	8	4	6
4	1	8	6	2	9	7	3	5
2	3	6	8	7	5	9	1	4
5	7	4	1	9	6	3	8	2
9	8	1	2	4	3	5	6	7
1	4	5	9	3	2	6	7	8
3	2	7	4	6	8	1	5	9
8	6	9	5	1	7	4	2	3

SOLUTION - WINTER

Crossword

How many are there?

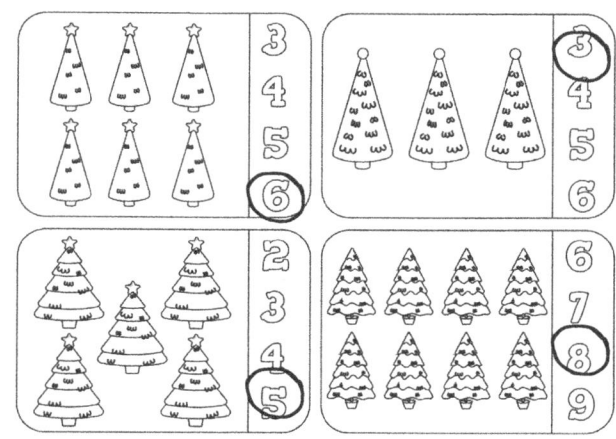

Starts with "C"

1. Christmas
2. Cookies
3. Cold
4. Chimney

find the same picture

fill in the blanks

PULLOVER   SOCK   HAT   SCARF   MITTEN

SOLUTION - WINTER

Weather matching

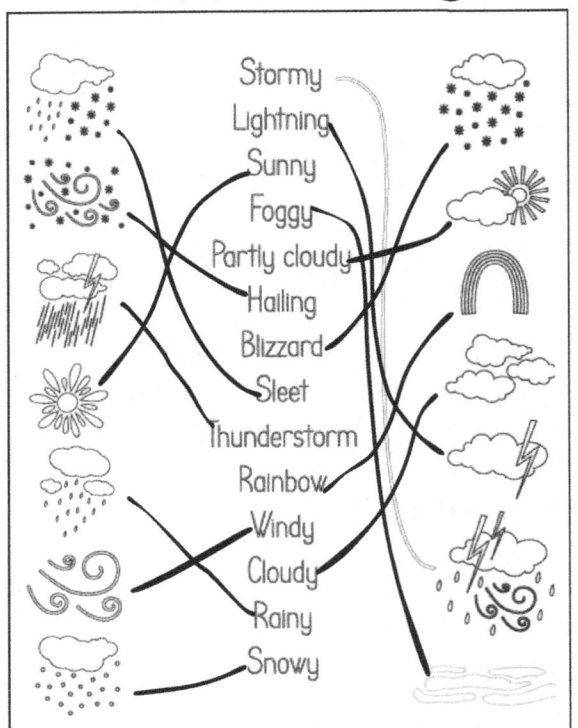

Stormy, Lightning, Sunny, Foggy, Partly cloudy, Hailing, Blizzard, Sleet, Thunderstorm, Rainbow, Windy, Cloudy, Rainy, Snowy

find the correct shadow

How many?

BROWN

| 3 | 3 | 2 |

BLUE

| 2 | 2 | 5 |

find the correct shadow

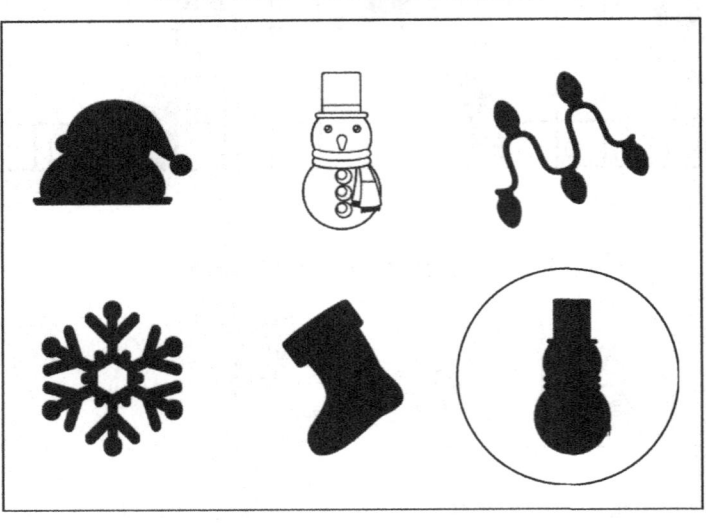

find the correct shadow

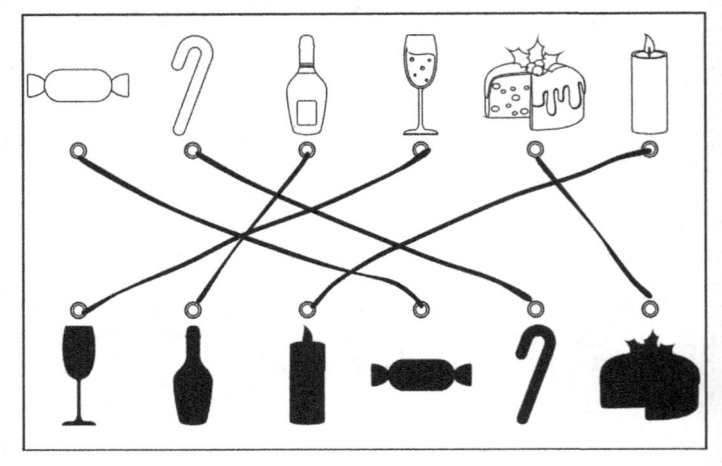

SOLUTION - WILD ANIMALS

lly sentence:

1. No action to protect wildlife is too small, every action is meaningful.
2. The savannas of Africa are populated by lions, cheetahs, and hyenas, engaged in a perpetual struggle for survival.
3. Tigers, known for their distinctive striped coats, are among the largest cats in the world.
4. The lush forests of the Pacific Northwest are home to grizzly bears, bald eagles, and salmon.

Word Search

Crossword

Sudoku

1	9	2	4	8	5	6	7	3
4	7	6	9	2	3	1	8	5
8	3	5	7	6	1	2	9	4
2	4	9	3	7	8	5	1	6
7	5	1	2	4	6	9	3	8
6	8	3	5	1	9	7	4	2
3	2	7	6	9	4	8	5	1
9	1	4	8	5	2	3	6	7
5	6	8	1	3	7	4	2	9

Match words with correct picture

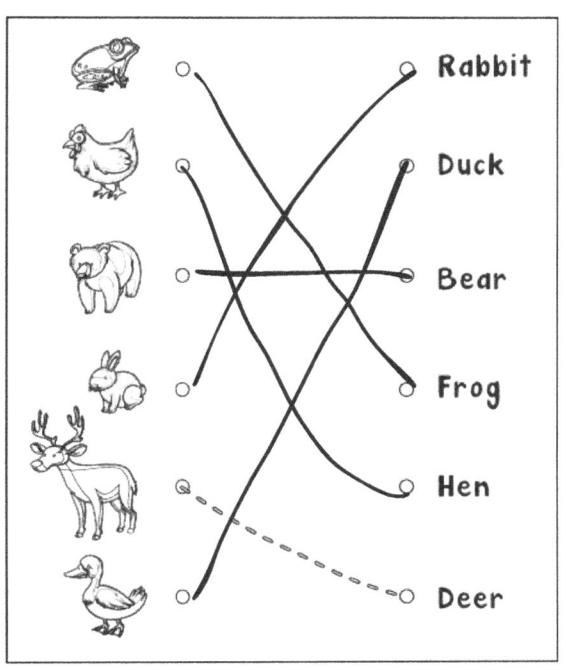

SOLUTION - WILD ANIMALS

Find the largest number

15	79	54	27	83	74	92	97	29	17
73	45	19	85	23	82	32	52	68	86
91	22	31	67	14	87	21	80	25	94
24	50	44	28	64	53	46	18	84	60
95	16	81	20	**98**	30	77	90	96	26

What is this:
1. Kangaroo
2. Shark
3. Chameleon
4. Dog
5. Eagle.

Fill in the blanks

Lion Deer
Cat Butterfly
Gorilla Horse
Hen Crab
Rat Turtle

Join the words

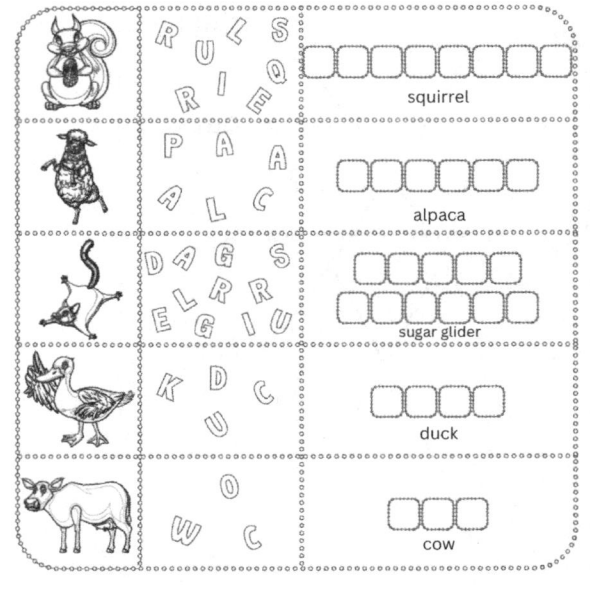

squirrel

alpaca

sugar glider

duck

cow

matching game

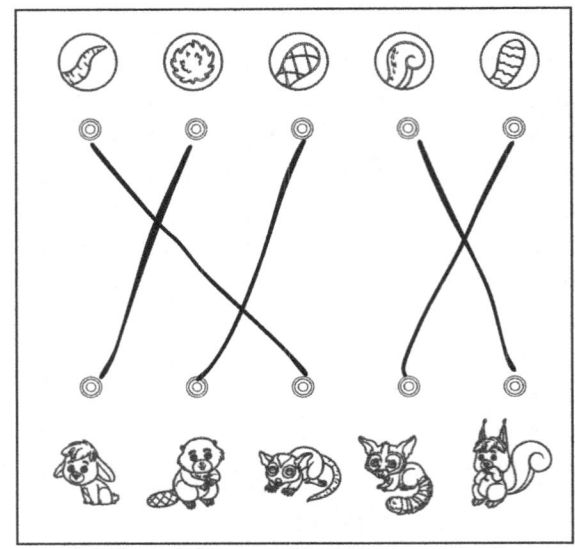

match correct pictures

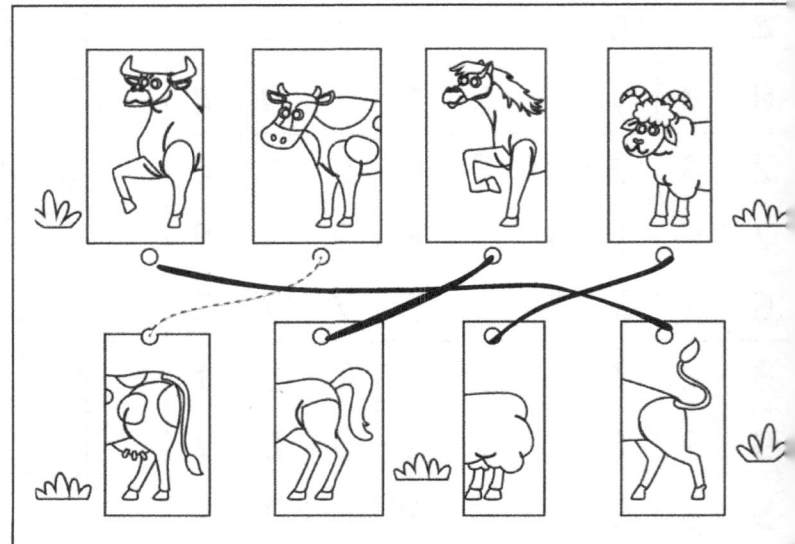

106

SOLUTION - WILD ANIMALS
find the correct shadow

4-6

How many

Dear Readers,

We would like to extend our heartfelt gratitude to you for taking the time and dedication to explore the book "Memory Training Riddles for Seniors". We hope that you have found both benefits and joy within its pages, and that the knowledge and skills from this book will continue to play an important role in your daily lives.

We want to express special thanks to those who have contributed, supported, and dedicated themselves to the creation of this book. The efforts and dedication of everyone involved have helped us to complete this product, from research to editing and design.

Finally, we hope that this book will serve as a useful tool in maintaining and enhancing memory and mental flexibility for seniors. We sincerely thank you and wish you good health, happiness, and enjoyment of life's wonderful moments.

With warm regards,

Made in the USA
Coppell, TX
24 January 2025

44718009R00063